Create His Kingdom

Create His Kingdom

A Biblical Journey in Creativity

BROOKE HARRIS

RESOURCE *Publications* · Eugene, Oregon

CREATE HIS KINGDOM
A Biblical Journey in Creativity

Resource Publications
An Imprint of Wipf and Stock Publishers
199 W. 8th Ave., Suite 3
Eugene, OR 97401

www.wipfandstock.com

PAPERBACK ISBN: 979-8-3852-7333-1
HARDCOVER ISBN: 979-8-3852-7334-8
EBOOK ISBN: 979-8-3852-7335-5

VERSION NUMBER 031226

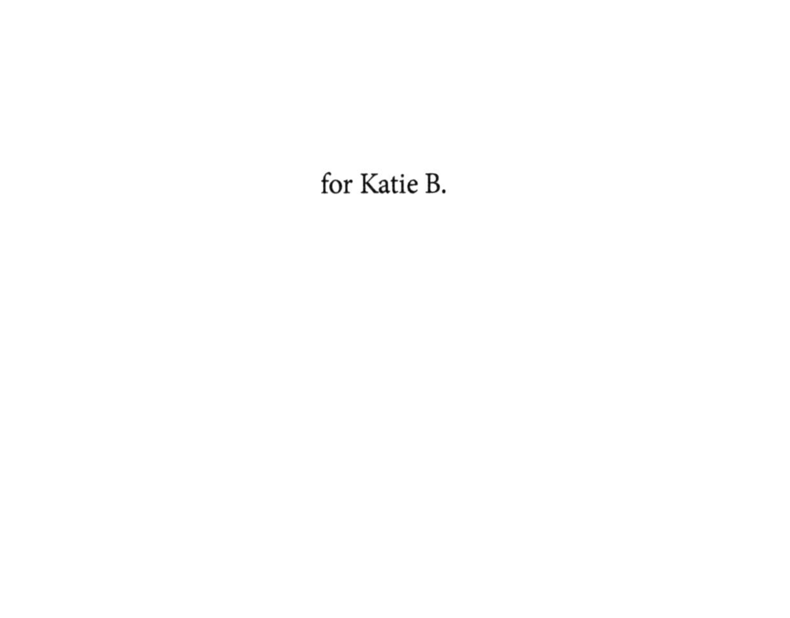

for Katie B.

Contents

List of Included Paintings/ Photographs

Preface

A Note from the Author

Dear Creative One,

As I wrote this study, I prayed for you. That might sound strange since I don't technically know most of you personally. I'm not familiar with your childhood experiences or the colors you tend to gravitate towards. I don't even know your name, but I know the God who does. It's this shared connection with our Heavenly Father that will guide us through this study.

My prayer is that you would grow closer to our Heavenly Father through His Spirit and that you would grow in confidence. Bloom into your true identity as a beloved child of God who has a special role to play in the kingdom. This Bible study is an introduction to a life where you get to do just that! I am excited that you have taken the steps to participate. God longs to speak to you, and I know He will meet you here.

Joyfully,

Brooke

Acknowledgements

Heartfelt appreciation goes out to the members and friends of St. Luke Church for their incredible support. Your own creative endeavors encourage me in mine.

Thank you to my husband, Aaron, who always supports my creative efforts. You keep me dreaming.

Thank you to my daughters, Kyla and Darah, who, through their multitude of art projects and Lego builds, help me remember to seek out creativity every day.

Thank you to my first readers: my dad, Ken Collins, and friend, Missy Rogers. Your feedback was invaluable and greatly helped shape the final product of this study. Thank you to my mom, Marilyn Collins, for participating in the first beta group!

Finally, thank you to my Creative Father, who called me to paint and, through creativity, led me to freedom.

How to Use This Study

Thank you for embarking on this unique journey with Create His Kingdom. This guided experience, spanning six sessions, is designed for personal exploration and growth. Each session, filled with scripture reading, reflection questions, and creative exercises, is a canvas for the Holy Spirit to stir your heart in unique ways. Each session is organized into six days, allowing participants to complete it within a week. Weeks are organized as follows:

Day 1–3: Discover

On these days, individuals will read scripture, commentary, and answer questions about the Bible reading and their own personal application.

Day 4: Creative Invitation

Day 4 is a special invitation for participants to connect with God in a personal, creative way. Whether it's through journaling or a simple creative exercise, this day is all about fostering a unique bond with God the Creator.

Day 5: Truths and Reflection

Day 5 writings invite readers to declare truths they have learned throughout the session and reflect personally on where God is at work in their lives. These questions and answers are for the person and the Lord.

Day 6: Group Reflection

Each group meeting will consist of prayer, a guided discussion, and a creative exercise. These fellowship questions may be answered and shared with the group. Leaders will facilitate this time of creativity. (See Leader's Guide for more information.)

About Creative Group Experiences

Each live meeting will include a creative activity that allows participants to engage. The purpose of the activity is for each person to encounter their Creator God through His Holy Spirit. This may be different and new for many but pray that the Lord will guide the participants and that they will encounter him. The list of supplies and each activity was kept simple on purpose so a creative encounter can be experienced even in the simplest of terms. Many of the activities require repeated items for ease of use.

For some of the art materials, ask participants before the study starts if they have any of the supplies on hand. Many people have craft and art supplies. Put them to good use.

Local churches may also have supplies to borrow, including those used by Children's Ministries, which regularly utilize items such as watercolor paints, brushes, scissors, and paper.

Simple student-quality supplies are perfectly adequate for this study. The following Amazon list is a guide if the local church or participants do not already have supplies. The list also includes items that group members might like to purchase to use after the study is over. Items were selected with quality and cost in mind.

Visit the Create His Kingdom Art Supplies Amazon list for suggestions: https://shorturl.at/aJaEn

Where the Soul Rests **by Brooke Harris**

Session 1

Identity

Introduction

As a child, I played in the wooded backyard of neighborhood friends. My sister, friends, and I tore branches of honeysuckle and bent them among the low branches of trees to create a leafy canopy. We nestled metal dishware and tiny vases of flowers in our little home. After a few afternoons of play, we felt the surge of creativity to rip it all down and build it again. From what I remember, building and creating our playhouse was the most fun part.

In the winter, the cold temperatures shooed us into the unfinished basement, but we continued to play and build. Exposed beams and cement floors transformed into a little town, complete with a police station, library, and restaurant, all made with sheet walls and old blanket rugs. We spent hours creating our own little shops — writing menus on dry-erase boards and organizing our books and library checkout systems. Once we set it all up, we played for a while, pretending to run our town. (For excitement, there was always someone in trouble with the police). Then, the creativity surged, and we tore down the clothes-pinned sheets from the rafters and started fresh, rebuilding with new ideas and new roles.

Play and creativity as a child are as easy as breathing, but much less so now as an adult. You might not be sure what it looks like yet, but we all have a creative call in God's kingdom. This six-week journey will help you see your identity in Christ Jesus and your special place in his church. My prayer is that each person who embarks on this study not only discovers their identity in Christ but also flourishes creatively in the life God has given them.

As the study unfolds, be open to how the Lord is meeting you in your life. Give space for his Spirit to speak with you and for his holy Scriptures to impact you. This study is not just about reading and answering questions, but about deep personal reflection and growth.

Before we begin, take a few moments to answer the following questions:

Why did you say yes to this specific study?

What are you asking the Lord to do these next six weeks through this study?

Day 1: Discover

Read Genesis Chapters 1 & 2.

As you read, underline the word make or create.

How many times did the text use the words "make" or "create"?

Out of all the things God created, what strikes you the most? Is there a particular act of creation that is your favorite, or one you are most awestruck by?

Whenever I read the story of creation, I am struck by the very vastness of God. He creates the entire universe with a simple word spoken over emptiness. Just to give you a little perspective, if the Milky Way galaxy (the galaxy Earth is in) were the size of North America, then our entire solar system would fit into a coffee cup.[1] Yes, all the planets, the sun, and everything in your fifth-grade solar system diorama would fit into a space of about three inches. The vast and beautiful universe is constantly expanding and defies all practicality. It shows a big God full of glory.

Many things in our lives defy practical needs. I don't need to decorate my Christmas tree every year with strands of bright lights and dozens of sparkling ornaments, but I want to. I look forward to it all year. When my parents invite my family over on Monday nights for dinner, my mother can cook basic, nutritious meals of chicken and vegetables, and it would suffice. But instead, she uses her creativity to sauté apples and cinnamon and caramelizes

1. "Milky Way," Western Washington University Physics/Astronomy Dept., para. 1.

onions to smother over delicious meats. She bakes chocolate chip cookies in ramekins with warm vanilla ice cream melting on top. These things aren't necessities, but they are creative acts of love. To me, they are the examples of what makes life especially worth living.

There is more to life than just necessity. God knew that from the beginning. Does one need billions of light-years of space? Our very creation was birthed out of the abundance of his love for us. The very first way God shows us his love is creation. There is no scarcity during the seven days of creation. He creates an entire universe and calls it good. It is the first example of God's great glory and his worthiness to be praised. How very honored we are to be the ones he loves, who he created at the culmination of his masterpiece and who live in the goodness of what he has made.

Reflect upon the very vastness of God's glory (i.e., an ever-expanding universe).

What does this Creator God's love look like?

Acts of Creation

The term "create" is a verb that generally means to bring something into existence or to cause something to happen.[2] It involves the act of making, forming, or producing something that did not previously exist. Creation can take various forms, including the physical, intellectual, or artistic realms.

Below are some unique ways to be creative. Can you think of others?

2. "create," Merriam-Webster Dictionary.

- Language – spoken word, storytelling, learning a new language
- Writing – poetry, creative writing, journaling
- Photography
- Digital Art – graphic design, digital painting, 3D modelling
- Manipulation of Materials – painting, sculpting, woodworking, etc.
- Crafting – jewelry making, sewing or knitting, upcycling items for a new life
- Music – instrument playing, singing, songwriting, producing/remixing songs
- Movement of Body – dance, acting, improv, choreography
- Gardening – designing gardens and cultivating crops, flower arranging
- Cooking/Baking – creating meals, recipes, food presentation
- Party Planning – creating space for fellowship, entertainment
- Interior Decorating/Design – creating calming spaces, problem-solving solutions for living
- Programming and Coding – developing apps, games, and software
- Filmmaking

Add more you can think of:

- ______________________
- ______________________
- ______________________

Day 2: Discover

Reread Genesis 2:19–20.

What action is happening in these verses?

Is this action creative? Why or why not? (See list of Acts of Creation.)

Why do you think God had Adam name the animals?

The Hebrew word for create is "bara."[3] The word is found predominantly in these first chapters of Genesis when God creates. It emphasizes the importance of this action to God. It highlights his unique ability to bring the universe and all living things into being, effortlessly creating the universe by simply speaking it into existence.

In the ancient Near East, something existed when it was given its function. Then and only then, it had a purpose and life.[4] When God creates, he names the specific creation and assigns it a function within his creative order. He calls the light "day" and the darkness "night." He separates the water and the dry ground and finishes by calling them "seas" and "land."

3. Keener and Walton, *Cultural Backgrounds Study Bible*, 4.
4. Keener and Walton, *Cultural Backgrounds Study Bible*, 4.

When Adam names the animals, he partners creatively with God, and he also entirely enters the deeper purpose of his existence. God names him and he gets to name the animals, assigning each one its own function within God's creative order. Notice that Adam named all the animals, and they each served a specific purpose for the Lord's creation.

But even then, "no suitable helper was found (2:20b)." The Lord needed to create someone to fulfill the purpose in partnership with Adam in the garden. Thus, woman was formed. Creation was not complete without Eve.

Reread Genesis 1:26–27.

What do you think it means to be created in God's image?

The imago Dei is the Latin term that Christian theologians have identified here in Genesis chapter one. As humans, we are created in the image of God. Because of this, we possess inherent dignity, worth, and a special relationship with him.[5]

Your Heavenly Father created you, and therefore, you are creative. You can see it in the early chapters of Genesis with Adam naming the animals and in humanity's rich history of art and culture. People made in his image are creative and bring forth life into his creation.

In what ways are you creative? Think outside the box. This doesn't have to mean artistic (which can be defined as creating with a specific medium).

Our identity lies deep in this story of Eden. We were not created out of necessity. God does not need us, but he wants us to join

5. Arnold, "Genesis," 5.

him to bring in his kingdom. He chooses to move at our speed with human interactions to bring about his goodness on Earth. He partnered with Moses and Aaron to bring the Hebrew people out of Egypt. He sent Jonah to warn and, therefore, rescue the people of Nineveh. He invited Adam to name the animals. Jesus showed himself to Mary in the garden so she could run and tell the others that he lives. Our God did not have to partner with any of these people for his purposes, but he did anyway. Why? Because he wants us. He loves us and longs to have a relationship with us. We are his children. Our purpose is to love and be loved by our Creator Father. We are not needed, but we are very much wanted.

What is the difference between being needed and wanted?

Day 3: Discover

Read 1 John 3:1–3 and Romans 8:15–17

John says our Father loves us so much, he calls us what?

John also says we are not shown yet what it will be like when Christ returns, but what do we know? What are we promised?

In Romans 8:15–17, it states that we are no longer fearful slaves to God. What are we instead?

What does it mean to be heir to something?

We are created in the image of God, and through God's grace and Jesus' sacrifice, we are transformed into the likeness of Christ. The word Christian means "little Christ." We are little Christs to the world. His Spirit moves through us and our identity in him.

Because we are created in his image, we are creative because he was first creative. Isn't creating one of the first things we do as children? We draw prolific collections of crayon and construction paper masterpieces. It is who we are. We are creators. The first part of our identity gets lost on the path to adulthood. So often, our creativity is stifled along the way, robbing us of our human identity and our connection to God.

An example of this is shown through a test commissioned by NASA to explore the nature of creativity. Scientists conducted a series of tests with a group of children over a decade, starting when the children were five years old. The researchers gave them puzzles to solve and assessed their creative problem-solving abilities using a strict criterion. At age five, 98 percent of the children were rated as creative geniuses. By age fifteen, the percentage dropped to only 12 percent. This moves to roughly 2 percent in adults.[6] In those ten years, creative identities were lost.

Think back to when you were a child (ages five to ten). What did you enjoy doing?

6. Medium, "The End of Education."

Day 4: Creative Invitation

Take a deep breath and invite the Holy Spirit to guide you in this creative exercise. Pray for all distractions inside you and in your environment to cease.

There are two blank pages following this invitation. Write the word "Jesus" in large print in the middle of the first page. Around it, write the descriptors and names for Jesus. You are simply answering this question: In your personal experience, who is Jesus?

After a few minutes, move to the second page and, in large print, write your name in the middle. Have the Holy Spirit guide you and ask Jesus this question: "Who do you say that I am"?

Write down the descriptors and nouns that he gives you for this question. This may not seem easy at first. You might hear something that seems strange or impossible but write it down anyway. Listen and place your identity in Jesus. You have the mind of Christ. You know him and can listen to his voice (John 10:27).

Day 5: Truths and Reflection

Truths for Declaring:

Each session includes a list of truths learned that week in our study. I invite you to declare them (out loud!) over yourself each day as you study. They are written in the first person so that you can do so.

1. I am creative because my Heavenly Father is creative (Gen 1:26–27).
2. I am a beloved child of the Most High God (2 Cor. 6:18).
3. Through Jesus' sacrifice, I am an heir of God's kingdom (Rom. 8:15–17).

Questions for You and the Lord

After reading through God's word and his truths this week, take a moment to reflect on the following questions. These questions are for you and God alone, unless you feel inclined to share them as an encouragement to others.

What truths do you easily believe this week? Why?

What truths this week are especially difficult to believe? Why? Have a conversation with your Heavenly Father about it. What in your past is clouding your future?

Day 6: Group Reflection

Group Discussion Questions

As you prepare for your meeting together, answer the following questions to share with the group.

Were there any study questions from Days 1–3 that stood out to you that you would like to discuss?

What is something you want to share with a friend from what you learned this week?

Think back to your answer of how you are creative. Share it with the group.

How do you make time for creativity in your life?

Creative Group Experience

Your leader will guide you in a creative exercise as a group. After completing the activity, you will be led to journal responses and to discuss:

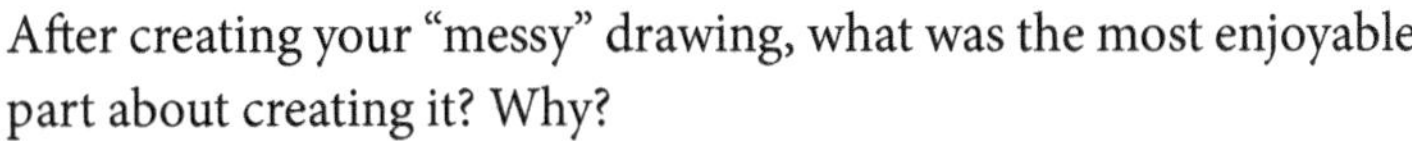

After creating your "messy" drawing, what was the most enjoyable part about creating it? Why?

Did the act of layering lots of different colors, patterns, and textures feel freeing or overwhelming? Why?

How would you act differently if you walked every day of your life with a complete sense of God wanting you as his child?

Leader, please see Session 1 Creative Group Experience in the Leader's Guide for instructions.

Close-up of *Echoes of Joy* by Brooke Harris

SESSION 2

Connection with God

Introduction

Part of my testimony is that for many years of my life, I was aware of God, but I did not honestly know him. I grew up in the church with a father who was a seminary professor. My parents were diligent in teaching me the tenets of Christianity, including the creeds and commandments. Through this, I knew him with my head, but not yet with my heart.

Over the years, through his gracious acts and several impactful encounters, I have developed a deeper relationship with Christ. I know him with my heart and head (even though my journey is long from finished!) Acts of creativity connect us to the Father, allowing us to hear his voice and know his heart. It breaks down the distractions of this world and the clutter in our minds. A creative act is a connection.

That is one of the main reasons I enjoy creating. As we create, we place ourselves in a posture to listen to our Father through his Holy Spirit. We can hear his voice clearly through an act of creation.

When people talk about hearing the voice of God, specific concerns pop up:

- Is this person for real?
- Do they really hear the voice of God?
- Are they crazy?

Inevitably, insecurities rise to the surface:

- I don't hear from the Lord.
- Is something wrong with me?
- Why don't I hear the voice of God like my friend/family member/coworker?
- I try to listen, but I don't hear anything!

To answer all these worries simply, God is much more concerned with our hearts than with how well we hear him. If we have the desire to know and love him, he will meet us there. The practice of listening to his voice is an important one and takes, well, practice. Everyone hears from him in different ways (see the text below titled Four Ways to Hear God's Voice), but the voice is the same yesterday, today, and forever (Hebrews 13:8). He wants to speak with you. He doesn't hide himself from his children, who are eager to listen.

Four Ways to Hear God's Voice

Much like we have different learning styles (visual, auditory, kinesthetic), there are distinct ways the Lord shares himself with us. Here are four main ways people hear God's voice. You might be gifted in all four or have one primary tendency. Often, as people go through various stages of their lives, God speaks to them in different ways.

Hearer

Natural Ability: Hearers have a natural ability to listen. They can hear through the distractions of life.

How God Communicates: Hearers can hear the voice of God audibly or as an inner voice. Many journal and hear the voice of the Lord constantly. This can be a clear message or guidance for others. Hearers need to ask the Lord, "Who is this word for"? as they often may hear snippets that don't reveal a complete picture.[1]

Biblical Examples:

- Samuel: As a child, Samuel heard God calling his name while he was sleeping in the temple (1 Sam 3:1–10).

1. Galloway, "Hearing God's Voice."

- Philip: The apostle Philip heard the voice of an angel giving him instructions to follow the road to Gaza. This later led him to meet and evangelize the Ethiopian eunuch (Acts 8:26–29).
- Practice: Ask the Lord for help processing the pieces of a larger picture. Intercede for others based on what you hear.

Feeler

Natural Ability: Feelers have big hearts and feel big feelings. The Lord uses this to show his compassion for others.

How God Communicates: God allows Feelers to know his heart and to feel his emotions. They often show compassion and empathy towards others in profound ways that surpass human will. They may be able to sense an environment as one that has a sense of peace, love, or warmth, and feel a sense of God's presence.[2]

Biblical Examples:

- David: Throughout the Psalms, David expresses a deep emotional connection with God, reflecting a range of feelings from joy to despair (Pss 23, 27, 51, 139).
- Mary, the mother of Jesus: After the angel Gabriel visits her, Mary expresses her joy in song, demonstrating deep spiritual maturity and emotion (Luke 1:46–55).
- Practice: Ask the Lord to help you sort through your own personal emotions and reveal his thoughts and feelings for the person or situation. The question is: Jesus, if you were physically in the room, how would you show this person love?

2. Galloway, "Hearing God's Voice."

Knower

Natural Ability: Knowers follow their intuitions. Often, they are the people who trust their instincts when making decisions.

How God Communicates: Knowers receive insights or knowledge from God. This can be explained by the phrase: 'they know that they know that they know.' Knowers tend to feel like the least spiritual people in the room. The way they hear God is less flashy, as it is not usually with words or images, but they are steady people of faith.[3]

Biblical Examples:

- Solomon: Solomon received the gift of wisdom from God. He was able to discern what God's justice and mercy looked like in various situations, including the story of the two women claiming to be the mother of the same baby (1 Kgs 3:16–28).
- John the Baptist recognized Jesus and declared him to be the Lamb of God. He listened to God and understood his role in preparing the way for Christ (John 1:29).
- Practice: Ask the Lord if it is him speaking or your intuition in situations. Pray for God to help you know his thoughts as your thoughts.

Seer

Natural Ability: Seers can be visual people with strong imaginations.

How God Communicates: Seers perceive the voice of God through visions, images, or symbolic representations that can convey spiritual messages. This could be through dreams or visions (awake dreams). Sometimes they see images in their mind as metaphors for what is happening in their situation.[4]

3. Galloway, "Hearing God's Voice."
4. Galloway, "Hearing God's Voice."

Biblical Examples:

- Ezekiel: Ezekiel had several visions, including the famous vision of the valley of dry bones, which symbolizes the restoration of Israel (Ezek 37:1–14).
- John the Apostle: In Revelation, John recounts a series of symbolic visions about the end times (Rev 4:1 onwards).
- Practice: As people share conversations about their lives, ask the Lord to give you a picture of them. You do not always need to share this, unless the Holy Spirit prompts you to do so. Practice seeing these images and metaphors and how they show God's love for the people you meet.

Day 1: Discover

Let's explore the truths the Bible teaches us to combat our insecurities about not being able to hear him. Joel Case wrote a great article discussing these barriers in Cultivated Journal Vol. 1.[5] Here are a few of the common ones we as humans combat:

Roadblock One

That was just me thinking those things, not God speaking…

Truth

"…we have the mind of Christ (1 Cor 2:16, NIV)."

If you have confessed with your mouth that Jesus is Lord, then he lives inside of you. Your thoughts are his thoughts. With practice, you will understand what thoughts are from him and which are your own. His Spirit convicts but never condemns. He encourages us to go deeper with him. Knowing the distinction between our heart and God's heart is a lifelong journey. Don't give up!

Roadblock Two

Trying to hear the voice of God and journal in his voice is too risky because it is subjective, and we have the Holy Scriptures anyway. It diminishes the Bible as the authority and could lead us astray.

Truth

"My sheep hear my voice, and I know them, and they follow me (John 10:27, ESV)."

5. Case, "Common Barriers," 22–25.

The simple answer to this roadblock is that this isn't how Jesus lived or how he directed others to live. Jesus knew the Holy Scriptures backwards and forwards and applied their teachings to his daily life, but he was also in non-stop communication with the Father. He prayed continually and told his disciples what his Father had said to him. He didn't do anything unless he heard the command from the Father first. During his last days on Earth, he begged the father to take the cup from him. Then Jesus listened to his father and knew he must do his father's will, rather than relying on his own fears and understanding.

Let's reverse the logic here. If we don't want to hear from the Lord any way other than Scripture, then why do we pray? We don't simply pray to a wall. We are connecting with our Lord who loves us. We wait in expectation for him to respond.

Mother Teresa did a rare 60 Minutes interview with Dan Rather back in the nineties, and when asked, "What do you say to God [when you pray]?" she replied, "I don't say anything, I listen."[6] Let us be like Mother Teresa and take the posture of a listener. God is at work in his creation. We must listen and be on the lookout for his goodness.

The enemy wants to keep us deaf to the Lord's voice, as connection with him is life-giving. Fiona Horrobin writes: "I have discovered the enemy wants to keep people in a straitjacket of rationale or even religion, when God is far bigger than all these and he is truly out of the box of our thinking."[7]

Listening to God's voice is the difference between our head knowledge about God and our heart knowing him personally. We can be confident that the voice we are listening to will align with the Bible.

6. Tipp City Church of the Nazarene, "Mother Teresa on Prayer."

7. Horrobin, *Healing through Creativity*, 173.

Roadblock Three

I'm afraid to journal God's voice. What if he punishes me?

Truth

"Therefore, there is now no condemnation for those who are in Christ Jesus (Rom 8:1)."

Horrobin continues: "The lie is that the ugliness inside must never come out, that it is too shameful to bring up. But that is the very place the Lord wants to heal us and release us."[8]

I invite you to journal and listen to your Heavenly Father. He knows your thoughts already. Why not share them with him in an act of vulnerability that can bring peace and understanding?

Follow in the footsteps of C.S. Lewis and what he said of prayer: "We must lay before him what is in us, not what ought to be in us."[9]

Reflection Questions

Which roadblock is the hardest for you when hearing the voice of God? Do you have challenges with another one not listed?

Reflect on a time in your life where you felt God's presence. How could you tell he was speaking to you? What was he saying?

8. Horrobin, *Healing through Creativity*, 195.

9. Lewis, *Letters to Malcolm*, 22.

Day 2: Discover

Read Psalm 46:10.

Is this verse familiar to you? Which part?

What does it mean in your life to "be still and know" that the Lord is God? What does it look like?

What does it look like for God to be exalted "among the nations… [and] in the Earth"? Is this happening now? What still needs to happen for this to be a reality?

We tend to stop at the first part of this verse — Be still and know that I am God — but the second is equally as important. The Lord will be exalted among the nations. It is a good reminder to maintain a posture of reverence before the Lord. Tyler Staton, in his book on prayer, says: "Be still. Remember who God is. Remember who you are. Then do your best to live without getting the order mixed up. That'll be enough."[10] Place him at the center where he belongs.

The frenetic pace of our world pressures us to constantly be doing something, to be connected to our phones, and to have an endless list of things to accomplish. Usually, that list is full of commitments that, if a real crisis came, wouldn't matter in the slightest. He is waiting for you.

10. Staton, *Praying Like Monks, Living Like Fools*, 49–50.

The pace keeps quickening. Due to technological advances, a 1965 Senate subcommittee predicted that Americans would work only fourteen hours a week by the year 2000, with at least seven weeks of vacation time. Well, they were right about one thing. Technological progress has made workers more productive than ever before. But rather than cutting back, we've added.[11]

The addition of modern overwhelm affects us so profoundly that when we enter a moment of silence, we struggle to focus. Our mind wanders to our to-do list and to our distractions.

I don't bring all of this up to lower our view of humanity, but this is a battle we are constantly fighting. Use heavenly tools of silence, prayer, and acts of creation to combat it. I invite you to cultivate the holy habit of silence, which brings healing and wholeness.

Read Jeremiah 33:3.

What does the Lord ask us to do in the first part of this verse?

What does it say he will do in response?

What are some examples of "unsearchable things you do not know"?

11. Sopher, "Where the FiveDay Workweek Came From."

What does this say about God's character?

This verse shows an amazing gift God gives us. We call on God and he answers us and tells us great things that we could never comprehend on our own. Now, I don't think this means I'll understand the time-space continuum anytime soon. However, this has already been theorized by many scientists. It has been searched.

But the greatness of God and his character know no bounds. When we call on him, he reveals pieces of himself to us so that we can see his great love for us.

Yes, God is mysterious, and no human will ever fully understand him, but he is not hiding from us. He shares great things with us freely when we listen.

Day 3: Discover

Read John 10:1–15.

Look at verse 3. In Jesus' illustration, how does the Shepherd call his sheep?

How do the sheep respond?

In this passage, Jesus speaks to the Pharisees, explaining who he is. What are some reasons they are unable to listen? (See John 10 as a whole.)

How does this passage personally relate to your relationship with Jesus?

God comes to each of us in our own unique context of life — our personality and culture. As we listen and look for his interactions with us, his presence and voice will become more apparent in our lives.

John Mark Comer, in his sermon "Listening to God," shares ways to hear God's voice, like sheep to a shepherd:[12]

12. Comer, "Listening to God."

Jesus himself

Jesus is the Word, present at creation. Hearing God's voice begins and ends with Jesus. All the other ways God communicates come through Jesus and point back to him.[13]

"Long ago God spoke many times and in many ways to our ancestors through the prophets. And now in these final days, he has spoken to us through his son. God promised everything to the Son as an inheritance, and through the Son, he created the universe. The Son radiates God's own glory and expresses the very character of God, and he sustains everything by the mighty power of his command (Hebrews 1:1–3, NLT)."

Scripture

God comes to the minds and imaginations of human writers. As we read the Scriptures, we obey and follow God. There are many ways to approach Scripture, including Lectio Divina, a way monks have used for centuries to connect with God.[14] This Latin phrase translates to "divine reading."

Steps:[15]

1. Lectio (Reading): Carefully read a biblical passage or text.
2. Meditatio (Meditation): Reflect on the text and its meaning.
3. Oratio (Prayer): Respond to the text in prayer.
4. Contemplatio (Contemplation): Rest in God's presence, often leading to a deeper awareness of him.

We don't want to manipulate the Bible; we aren't asking for a new meaning. We ask the Holy Spirit what part of the original meaning he wants to highlight in our own lives.

13. Comer, "Listening to God."
14. Comer, "Listening to God."
15. Gaultiere, "How to Do Lectio Divina."

Circumstances

Many people stop with Jesus and Scripture, but the God who created the universe is still active in our world. He still speaks, and he does this through our circumstances. God is present in the actions and opportunities in our lives and leads and guides us to a deeper relationship with him. Limitations, struggles, situations, talents, and skills are all areas in which God uses us to call us to him and his will.

Our Desires

We can discern God's voice by listening carefully to the desires of our hearts and seeing if they align with God's character. This is not a "be true to yourself" cultural doctrine. The desires of our hearts can be the mark of a journey to who God creates us to be. Check these desires against God's character and his Scripture.

The question is: Where is the Spirit of God coming through my own heart?

The Prophetic

Dreams and visions are another way God speaks to us. God also speaks to us through one another. The body edifies each part.

A simple way to do this is to take a moment of silence before you pray for someone and ask the Lord to open your imagination to pray for them. You may come up with a word or picture that you can share with them humbly. They can test this against Scripture and community.

Listening Prayer

This prayer is waiting quietly for God to speak into your mind and heart. Because we have the mind of Christ, God has access to our thoughts, imagination, and hearts. God guides our thoughts when we are willing to listen.

The Spirit of God dwells inside of you, so of course he is able to speak to your thoughts and mind. He can offer you ideas that can direct your entire life. Test them against Jesus' teachings.

Day 4: Creative Invitation

Developed from a prompt from Tyler Staton's book, Praying Like Monks, Living Like Fools:[16] Set a timer for two minutes so you will not be distracted by wondering how much time has passed.

The goal is not to hear the voice of the Lord or expect revelation. It might happen, and it is exciting! But these two minutes of silence are an offering to the Lord — our submission to him in his glory to "be exalted among the nations (Ps 46:10)." We are exalting him in our spirits and in our lives, two minutes at a time. After your two-minute offering, read the following poem as a prayer.

Yielding

by Abbi Bodager

Lord, help me yield.

Not to this spiraling

circus that boils my brain,

but to winter, summer, autumn,

spring, to holy pruning.

I surrender my ruptured

senses, my subtle addictions.

Teach me to love, to see,

to stroll with You in the cool

of the dawn.

16. Staton, *Praying Like Monks, Living Like Fools*, 50–51.

Meet a Fellow Creator: Abbi Bodager

Abbi is a poet and student who passionately creates in a variety of art forms, but especially storytelling. She loves to write poems with themes of faith, beauty, and finding hope during pain. You can read more of her work at: https://substack.com/@heavensdeclare.

Day 5: Truths and Reflection

Truths to Declare

Each session includes a list of truths learned that week in our study. I invite you to declare them (out loud!) over yourself each day as you study. They are written in the first person so that you can do so.

1. I am a sheep and Jesus is my Shepherd. I know his voice (John 10:4–5).
2. God loves me and does not condemn me. His Spirit corrects and encourages (Rom 8:1; John 14:26).
3. When I call on the Lord, he answers (Jer 33:3).

Questions for You and the Lord

After reading through God's Word and his truths this week, take a moment to reflect on the following questions. These questions are for you and God alone, unless you feel inclined to share them as an encouragement to others.

What truths do you easily believe this week? Why?

In what ways do you distract yourself from time with God?

How will you use creative tools to help you listen to his voice?

Day 6: Group Reflection

Group Discussion Questions

As you prepare for your meeting together, answer the following questions to share with the group:

Were there any study questions from Days 1–3 that stood out to you that you would like to discuss?

What is something you want to share with a friend from what you learned this week?

Reflect on the roadblocks to hearing God's voice. Which one do you struggle with? Is there another one not listed that impacts you?

Refer to the section, Listening to God's Voice. In which way do you naturally feel led to listen to him?

Creative Group Experience

Your leader will guide you in a creative exercise as a group. After completing the activity, your leader will guide you to journal responses to the following questions:

What colors did you choose for your emotions, and why?

Did your colors blend or touch? What about that did you like or dislike?

Was there anything significant in the act of creating that struck you?

Emotionally, what feelings are blending and confusing for you?

Leader, please see Session 2 Creative Group Experience in the Leader's Guide for instructions.

Quiet Beneath the Noise by Brooke Harris

SESSION 3

Community

Introduction

My oldest daughter, who is ten at the time of writing this book, was recently sick with strep throat. It is a widespread and treatable illness. As I drove away from the pharmacy with her antibiotics, I gave a prayer of thanks and thought of the church, which may seem like a strange idea, but here is the thread:

My daughter was suffering from a very curable illness, but without a community of healthcare providers, she would not have gotten well. If I had not driven her to the pediatrician's office, if the nurse had not swabbed her throat to test for strep, if the doctor had not examined her and prescribed her medicine, if the pharmacist had not filled her prescription, she would not be well.

That's the way it is in God's family as well. The church, Christ's body of believers, is a community that relies on one another for support. We are dependent on God's grace through Jesus' sacrifice, and we testify his goodness to others.

I have had many Christ-followers in my life who have encouraged me, challenged me, and shown me the love of God. This week, as you move through Session 3, I invite you to explore the church's role in each other's healing and the world's. Before we get started into our Scripture reading,

How would you define the word community?

Day 1: Discover

Read Isaiah 61 and Luke 4:17–21.

What does it say the Lord will do in Isaiah 61:2?

Reread Isaiah 61:1–2 and Luke 4:17–19. What is the significance of Jesus' reading this section of Isaiah in the synagogue?

Describe what God gives to his people in Isaiah 61.

Isaiah 61 demonstrates that justice with mercy blooms righteousness. Without God, humans err too harshly, or too leniently with the seriousness of sin. God is the perfect balance as his Spirit moves us to righteousness.

At the start of his ministry, immediately after Jesus returns from the wilderness with the power of the Holy Spirit, he visits the synagogue in his hometown and stands to read the Scriptures. And then, as he closes the scroll, he says, "The Scripture you've just heard has been fulfilled this very day! (Luke 4:21 NLT)."

Mic drop. Jesus just revealed himself as the Messiah! Except that if you read on, what happens? His hometown family and neighbors scoff at him and say, "Isn't this Joseph's son? He isn't anyone special."

But Jesus knew his identity. He knew how to listen to the voice of his father. He also knew the long and suffering road to the cross was coming. It was a path with purpose. Fulfilment of the Scriptures as the one true Messiah is glorious, but the road to complete that plan was a humbling and excruciating one.

Jesus is head of the church; we are his body, the ones he came to save. He grafted us into the line of Abraham, bringing together Gentiles and Jews, so that we might share in the grace of our Lord Jesus Christ. What a fantastic gift this is!

Tomorrow we will look at the church and its role. For now, reflect on the question below.

Jesus is the true Messiah and the head of the church. By God's grace, we are being transformed into his likeness.

What does this look like specifically in your life?

Day 2: Discover

Read Eph 4:11–16.

What is another name for the body of Christ?

Who is the head of the body? (vs. 15)

In these verses, how many times is the word "we" used?

Verse 16 states that each part of the church performs its own exceptional work and helps other parts grow and develop. How do you think creativity plays a role in the church?

As Christians, we often quote the phrase from Ephesians 4:15, "speak truth in love." What do you think that looks like? How is it accomplished well?

Let's first notice that in this Ephesians passage, the word "we" is used often. Just as there is no "I" in team, there is no "I" in church. We stand before God together, joined with our brothers and sisters in Christ, to do our own exceptional work full of love.

These verses might seem like a daydream to you, rather than the challenging experiences you've had within the church body. I, too, have experienced the pain of churches splitting and broken relationships. But I can't give up hope on the church.

I know many who have been hurt by the church, meaning hurt by "us." I long for Jesus' restoration in this area, but it will not come unless we are all united. We will not be united until we each reach out first, not with harsh truth or misguided love, but with truth in love. To me, the conflict of the church is part of our growing pains. Although very difficult, it is necessary so that we can be like the church in Ephesians 4:13 (NLT):

"This will continue until we all come to such unity in our faith and knowledge of God's Son that we will be mature in the Lord, measuring up to the complete standard of Christ."

We must strive to meet the full standard of Christ. Daunting, yes, but remember we are given his own Spirit who guides us and speaks for us when we have no words to utter. One day, the church will measure up to Christ, and she will be ready for his return. That takes growing pains and pruning.

Reflect on Isaiah 61 and the Messiah's role for his people. In the beginning of the chapter, the Lord comforts and saves those who are brokenhearted, grieving, and held captive. These people are in the most desperate position of their lives. They can only rely on the Lord in their terrible circumstances. At the end of this chapter, who are these people? The same people who were heartbroken and in the prison of their own shame are the ones in the end who will be dressed "with the clothing of salvation and draped in a robe of righteousness."

This is the church. This is us. We were enslaved in our own brokenness and sin, and Jesus rescued us. Not only did he rescue us, but he also continually forms us into his likeness so that we can show the world his love. We are moving from immaturity to maturity.

Fiona Horrobin writes: "God is raising his voice in our day in answer to the cries he hears. He has an answer for those in need, through the healing that is there for us all, through belonging to him and living as part of his family."[1]

The church lives as God's family.

My father gives an excellent analogy about the church of God. We are all small pieces of mosaic glass. You may look at the tiny piece of colored glass in your hand and think, "What good is this? How will this amount to anything"? But in the hands of our Creator Father, he places the pieces of glass in a beautiful arrangement. Each piece is set in a perfect position to form a large and beautiful mosaic that is the church.

You must just do your piece. Along the way, comparison and discontentment may seep in. We often look to our left and right and see what our brothers' and sisters' pieces are. We might be jealous of the way they are called to serve the Lord, but I encourage you to speak candidly with the Lord and your community about what your "piece" is. Who God created you to be is most special. He wants you to participate in bringing in his Kingdom the way he intended.

As the church, we must actively grow closer to Christ and to one another by "speaking truth in love" (Eph 4:15). As the body of believers, we are called to live and speak in a manner that demonstrates sincerity, kindness, and truthfulness.

Pray to God and ask: What is my role as part of the church? This could be how you serve in your church community, but also how you are showing others Christ Jesus outside the doors of your church.

1. Horrobin, *Healing through Creativity*, 27.

Day 3: Discover

Read Mark 5:25–34.

Before the woman was healed, what can you imagine were the ramifications of her blood disease as she lived in a Jewish culture?

What did Jesus heal the woman from?

How did her life change with God's healing?

The consequences of this woman's condition were grave. Under Jewish law, vaginal bleeding was considered unclean. Intercourse was not permitted during a woman's time of bleeding.[2] In Pharisaic tradition, it was common for couples to divorce if no children were born. Based on her age, this condition most likely either ended this woman's marriage or prevented her from having one.[3]

She also endured social isolation, as many must have avoided physical contact with her to prevent themselves from becoming ritually impure. She was alone, unable to visit her family and friends. She did not interact with people in public for fear of contaminating them. Bleeding for twelve years was a sentence to

2. Smith, "Mark," 599.
3. Keener and Walton, *Cultural Backgrounds Study Bible*, 1698.

solitary confinement, a life of isolation. The emotional and psychological strain of being ostracized from her community must have been terrible.

This woman also would not have been allowed in the temple to worship because of her ritual impurity.[4] Yet we know she continued to seek the Lord, because here she is reaching out for the cloak of the Messiah. Just as the Scriptures tell us in Malachi 4:2 (NLT):

"But for you who fear my name, the sun of righteousness shall rise with healing in its wings. You shall go out leaping like calves from the stall."

In her great suffering, this woman knew the Messiah to have healing in his wings — the wings of his prayer shawl — if only she could touch it...

And then Jesus walks past her.

He reverses all the ritual impurity and its complications that she endured for more than a decade. He heals her physically, emotionally, spiritually, and relationally. After her encounter with Jesus, she returns to her community, cleansed.

In Jewish Pharisaic tradition, if an unclean person touches a clean person, the clean person is considered impure.[5] The very opposite happens to the woman when she touches Jesus' garment. The impure becomes pure again. He restores her with righteousness. He makes her whole.

One of the most challenging parts of the woman's suffering with the blood condition was her loneliness. She was ostracized from her community.

We need one another, and we need community.

4. Keener and Walton, *Cultural Backgrounds Study Bible*, 1698.

5. Smith, "Mark," 599.

Like the woman with the blood condition, what do you need to be healed or restored from today? Ask the Lord to help you identify an area in your life that needs restoration and healing.

Who do you consider your community? Is it full or lacking?

Day 4: Creative Invitation

Use the space provided in this workbook and gather some colorful writing utensils. These could be colored pencils, markers, or crayons — whatever you prefer.

Using different colors, begin to draw small shapes on your page, leaving space in between each one like a mosaic. Don't second guess yourself. Silence the inner critic and simply draw for the act of it.

See how the edge of one shape forms the edge of another. Continue drawing the abstract colorful shapes close together like tiles. Notice what colors look good next to each other.

Reflect on the question from Day Two and ask the Lord: "What is my piece of your larger mosaic"? He could give you a specific skill or talent to develop for his sake. He could think of a particular group of people to serve. Say "yes" to his invitation to partner with him. Journal his response in the space provided:

Day 5: Truths and Reflection

Truths to Declare

Each session includes a list of truths learned that week in our study. I invite you to declare them (out loud!) over yourself each day as you study. They are written in the first person so that you can do so.

1. Because of Jesus, I am clothed in the Lord's righteousness (Isa 61:10).
2. I am a new creation! I am being transformed into the likeness of Christ every day (2 Cor 5:17).
3. I am part of Christ's church, and I am a special piece of his plan (1 Cor 12:12–27).

Questions for You and the Lord

After reading through God's word and his truths this week, take a moment to reflect on the following questions. These questions are for you and God alone, unless you feel inclined to share them as an encouragement to others.

What truths do you easily believe this week? Why?

What aspects of these truths would you like to explore more?

Ask the Lord what the next steps are for your "piece" that you bring to the church. Is there something he wants to show you about your role?

Day 6: Group Reflection

Group Discussion Questions

As you prepare for your meeting together, answer the following questions to share with the group:

Were there any study questions from Days 1–3 that stood out to you that you would like to discuss?

What is something you want to share with a friend from what you learned this week?

When was a time you felt the reassuring presence of God even when things were difficult? How did you experience it? Through prayer? Community? Healing?

Creative Group Experience

Your leader will guide you in a creative exercise as a group. After completing the activity, they will guide you to journal responses to the following questions:

What happened when the watercolors interacted with the white crayon?

Do you naturally gravitate toward community or solitude?

Where do you see yourself resisting the Holy Spirit?

How is the Holy Spirit calling you to the one that is not your natural bent?

Leader, please see Session 3 Creative Group Experience in the Leader's Guide for instructions.

Close up of *Where the Soul Rests* by Brooke Harris

SESSION 4

Healing

Introduction

For over ten years, my husband, Aaron, was a cardiac ICU nurse at a large regional hospital. There, he cared for the sickest patients from the surrounding areas. He later became what is known as an ECMO specialist, a highly-trained nurse who manages a life support device that essentially performs the functions of the heart and lungs. It pumps blood out of the body through long tubing, oxygenates it, and returns it to the patient. It is hoped to give the most critical patients time to recover until they are strong enough to be weaned off the machine. Unfortunately, patients on ECMO can decline and stay there for several months with no real signs of improvement. Patients receiving this support have a 50/50 survival rate at best.

With that dire outlook, it is common for doctors and medical professionals to see the signs of decline in patients and simply give up hope that they will ever get better.

One such patient was assigned to my husband. The patient was a man who was relatively healthy but suffered from a harmful lung infection, which left his lungs incapacitated. He had been on ECMO for weeks with no real signs of improvement. The doctors had run out of ideas.

With all other staff seeing the downward spiral, my husband stood by this man's hospital bed and prayed. The next day, the patient showed some improvement. He began to require less support from the numerous machines that assisted his bodily functions. Aaron prayed again for Jesus to receive the glory for this man's healing. The next day, the patient's health was stronger. He was more focused and able to carry on a conversation. Aaron prayed again for this man's complete healing.

The patient's health continued to improve. He was taken off ECMO and was able to breathe on his own. He recovered in another unit for a few days and then walked out of the hospital.

Healing

Jesus is the Great Physician and the ultimate Healer of our lives.

What healing have you received in your life?

Day 1: Discover

Read Isaiah 53 (The prophecy of Jesus — also called the "Suffering Servant" passage.)

What does verse three say Jesus is "familiar with"?

How does Christ's familiarity with suffering affect you today?

Verse 5 says, "the punishment that brought us peace was on him." In what ways did Jesus restore peace?

Verse 5 also says, "and by his wounds we are healed." In what ways can we be healed?

Verse 4 shows us that Christ was "punished by God." This is a serious matter, both today and in ancient times. This expression was used in ancient texts to describe an illness or accident that was explicitly believed to have been caused by the gods themselves.[1] Jesus bore the weight of our sin and took on the injury and death that was supposed to be ours. He endured extreme physical, emotional, and spiritual suffering.

1. Keener and Walton, *Cultural Backgrounds Study Bible*, 1829.

The Hebrew word for peace is "shalom", and it has a deeper meaning than "without conflict." Shalom is the complete restoration of wholeness and well-being. Through his death on a cross, Jesus redeems the relationship between God and humanity.

There are several interpretations of Isaiah 53:5 — "and by his wounds we are healed." Scholars agree that the focus of Chapter 53 is the salvation Christ offers through his sacrifice. His suffering and death have offered us healing from the consequences of sin and separation from God.

Other scholars, due to the physicality of the verse — "by his stripes," referring to the marks left by Jesus' scourging and torture — believe in the physical healing this verse promises. They believe Jesus' physical death is a path to holistic restoration.

In America, with our advancements in medicine, we don't witness the number of miraculous healings that other countries do. This does not mean miraculous healings do not exist. Jesus performed countless miracles of physical healing during his time on Earth.

"The blind see and the lame walk; the lepers are cleansed and the deaf hear; the dead are raised, and the poor have the gospel preached to them (Matt 11:5 NIV)."

Thousands witnessed Jesus as he healed the sick, cast out demonic spirits, raised people from the dead, and cured blindness, deafness, leprosy, and lameness. Indeed, Jesus had demonstrated that he is Lord over physical healing.

There are countless stories too in our modern medicine world, where tumors have disappeared, terminal cancer has dissipated, and people have come to life after being declared dead.

Christ's death paid for all sin and its consequences. All healing is available through Christ Jesus. He endured the suffering of dying on a cross, the turmoil of becoming a social outcast, and the pain of being abandoned by his loved ones. That suffering constitutes complete healing. His sacrifice is sufficient for complete restoration.

But Jesus always pointed to the deeper spiritual world, not just the physical.

When the Jews were worried about what they would eat, drink, and wear, Jesus assured them of the Father's love for them and that he would provide for their needs (Matt 6:25–27).

When the people were concerned with the physical overthrow of the Roman government and wanted to make Jesus their king, Jesus pointed to a greater spiritual truth — that following him leads to eternal life (John 6:47).

Jesus' sacrifice is sufficient for complete healing in all areas: physical, emotional, spiritual, and relational. I invite you to receive the fullness of his love and sacrifice.

Many have experienced Jesus as Friend, Lord, and Savior. Fewer have experienced him as Healer. I don't begin to say I know the will of God and why some suffer. This is one of the most difficult philosophical questions one can ask. But I do know that we need to pray in power. That healing is available to us through Christ Jesus.

We pray weak prayers for safety and comfort. Instead, let us specifically ask the Lord for healing by his power through the Holy Spirit. Pray in faith for his healing in your life — complete healing and restoration, including body, soul, mind, and spirit.

What would a prayer like that look like?

Day 2: Discover

Today, you are invited to focus on all aspects of healing. Please read the following passages of what Jesus offers in terms of healing:

Physical Healing

"He took her by the hand and said to her, 'Talitha koum!' (which means 'Little girl, I say to you, get up!'). Immediately, the girl stood up and began to walk around (she was twelve years old). At this, they were completely astonished (Mark 5:41–42 NIV)."

"'Go,' said Jesus, 'your faith has healed you.' Immediately, he received his sight and followed Jesus along the road (Mark 10:52 NIV)."

"Then Jesus said to the centurion, 'Go! Let it be done just as you believed it would' And his servant was healed at that moment (Matt 8:13 NIV)."

Emotional Healing

"Peace I leave with you; my peace, I give you. I do not give to you as the world gives. Do not let your hearts be troubled and do not be afraid (John 14:27 NIV)."

"The Spirit of the Lord is on me, because he has anointed me to proclaim good news to the poor. He has sent me to proclaim freedom for the prisoners and recovery of sight for the blind, to set the oppressed free (Luke 4:18 NIV)."

"When Jesus saw her weeping, and the Jews who had come along with her also weeping, he was deeply moved in spirit and troubled. 'Where have you laid him?' he asked. 'Come and see, Lord' they replied. Jesus wept (John 11:33–35 NIV)."

Spiritual Healing

"Jesus straightened up and asked her, 'Woman, where are they? Has no one condemned you?' 'No one, sir' she said. 'Then neither do I condemn you' Jesus declared. 'Go now and leave your life of sin (John 8:10–11 NIV).'"

"Jesus said to him, 'Today, salvation has come to this house, because this man, too, is a son of Abraham. For the Son of Man came to seek and to save the lost (Luke 19:9–10 NIV).'"

"Some men brought to him a paralyzed man, lying on a mat. When Jesus saw their faith, he said to the man, 'Take heart, son; your sins are forgiven' At this, some of the teachers of the law said to themselves, 'This fellow is blaspheming!'"

Knowing their thoughts, Jesus said, 'Why do you entertain evil thoughts in your hearts? Which is easier: to say, 'Your sins are forgiven,' or to say, 'Get up and walk'? But I want you to know that the Son of Man has authority on Earth to forgive sins.'"

So, he said to the paralyzed man, 'Get up, take your mat and go home (Matt 9:2–4 NIV).'"

Relational Healing

"As Jesus was getting into the boat, the man who had been demon-possessed begged to go with him. Jesus did not let him, but said, 'Go home to your own people and tell them how much the Lord has done for you, and how he has had mercy on you (Mark 5:18–19 NIV).'"

"Come, see a man who told me everything I ever did. Could this be the Messiah? (John 4:29 NIV)"

Again, Jesus said, 'Peace, be with you! As the Father has sent me, I am sending you' And with that, he breathed on them and said, 'Receive the Holy Spirit. (John 20:21–22 NIV).'"

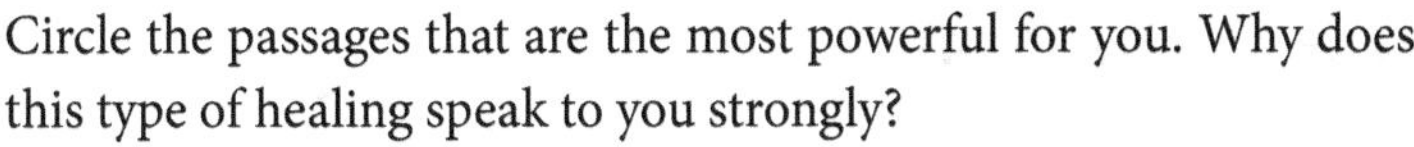

Circle the passages that are the most powerful for you. Why does this type of healing speak to you strongly?

What healing do you need from Jesus today?

Which type of healing do you find the hardest to ask for?

Day 3: Discover

Read John 11:17–43 (The Raising of Lazarus).

What is significant about how Jesus heals Lazarus?

In verse 24, what is Martha talking about with Jesus?

What is Jesus' reply?

This story encompasses many of the components of Jesus' complete healing. First, he emotionally and empathetically connects with Lazarus' sisters, Mary and Martha:

"Therefore, when Jesus saw her weeping, and the Jews who came with her weeping, He groaned in the spirit and was troubled. And he said, 'Where have you laid him?' They said to him, 'Lord, come and see.' Jesus wept (John 11:33–35 NIV)."

The grief of Mary and Martha moves him, and his weeping demonstrates both his human emotions and his connection to the people he loved. While he eventually raises Lazarus, his first response is to share in their sorrow. He also shows grief at death itself — because he knew death was never God's intended plan for his people.

After emotional healing and empathy, Jesus then proceeds to the physical healing:

"When he had said this, Jesus called in a loud voice, 'Lazarus, come out!' The dead man came out, his hands and feet wrapped with strips of linen, and a cloth around his face (John 11:43 NIV)."

Jesus miraculously heals Lazurus in front of a crowd of his family and other Jewish people for God's glory. Many ancient Jews believed that after three days the soul leaves the body, hence the significance of Lazarus being dead in the tomb for four days. By raising Lazarus on the fourth day, Jesus restores Lazarus' spirit to his body as well.

Not only was Lazarus physically restored, but the crowd also witnessed spiritual healing:

"I knew that you always hear me, but I said this for the benefit of the people standing here, that they may believe that you sent me (John 11:42 NIV)."

Lastly, Jesus restored the family relationship — brother and sisters reunited, able to follow him together.

Day 4: Creative Invitation

After the isolation of the COVID-19 pandemic, many have battled loneliness and depression. Fiona Horrobin, who runs a spiritual retreat center in Lancashire, England, has seen God use the creative arts to bring healing and freedom:

"Many people suffer deep anxiety because they have never been able to express their own personhood (positively or negatively) through their own free will. Healing of the will is a major part of the creative healing God wants to bring."[2]

Creativity frees people from the burden of "what should be done" and instead invites the question: "What do you want to do"?

Listen to Clair de Lune by Debussy (search on YouTube or any music app).

Be still before the Lord. Ask him to quiet your mind. Allow the music to wash over you.

What did you feel as you listened?

Was your body more relaxed afterwards?

What images came to mind?

2. Horrobin, *Healing through Creativity*, 99.

How do the arts create a space to connect with God?

Day 5: Truths and Reflection

Truths to Declare

Each session includes a list of truths learned that week in our study. I invite you to declare them (out loud!) over yourself each day as you study. They are written in the first person so that you can do so.

1. Jesus's sacrifice fully restores me to the Father (2 Cor 5:18–19).
2. By his stripes I am healed (Isa 53:4).
3. Jesus's healing is offered freely to me, and I can receive it wholeheartedly (Gal 2:20–21).

Questions for You and the Lord

After reading through God's word and his truths this week, take a moment to reflect on the following questions. These questions are for you and God alone, unless you feel inclined to share them as an encouragement to others.

What truths do you easily believe this week? Why?

What aspects of these truths would you like to explore more?

Ask the Lord: What are the next steps in my healing? Is there a place You want to reveal where I need restoration?

Day 6: Group Reflection

Group Discussion Questions

As you prepare for your meeting together, answer the following questions to share with the group.

Were there any study questions from Days 1–3 that stood out to you?

What is something you want to share with a friend from what you learned this week?

When was a time you experienced healing from the Lord? Was it physical, spiritual, or emotional?

Creative Group Experience

After your leader guides the activity, journal your reflections:

Which stanza did you like best in your composition, and why? Did it represent mind, body, or heart?

Which emotion was most difficult to express in words? Why?

How was it healing to write your emotions before the Lord?

Leader, please see Session 4 Creative Group Experience in the Leader's Guide for instructions.

A Pause Within by Brooke Harris

Session 5

Sabbath

Introduction

I remember the first few weeks after the birth of my oldest daughter. It was a fantastic time of newness, learning, and welcoming this little newborn girl into our family. What I didn't account for was the sheer exhaustion newborns bring. I had been warned, but I naively thought: Don't babies sleep a lot?

At the time, I taught online college writing classes, and since my daughter was born at the end of my five-week course, I thought I could complete the class and finish the necessary grading.

Boy, was I wrong. Instead of cherishing those first few weeks, I was drawn to complete hours of grading, a task I had given myself to do when I could have easily asked for help from other faculty members. I felt that I needed to uphold my end of the agreement and complete the course. In the end, I felt like a candle being burnt at both ends and in the middle.

In my night-feeding post-partum stupor, I graded things carelessly and was slow to respond to students, resulting in my lowest performance survey result as a teacher.

As I look back at this time, I realize I was in desperate need of rest. I believed the lie that I was too needed, and I would let people down by asking for help. While this was a specific season, it is a small example of what a life without rest looks like.

I often hear people in the same predicament I was in. They feel overwhelmed and busy, but they don't act. They acquiesce to the lie that this way of life is just the way it is.

If someone were to ask me, what spiritual discipline has impacted your life the most, out of all of them (fasting, scripture reading, prayer, etc.), I would choose Sabbath. How wonderful that we have a good Father who gives us rest and weaves it into the very creation he made for us!

I've had people express a desire for Sabbath, but they just don't know how to achieve it. I compare a life without Sabbath to this: it is like planning a fantastic vacation with your family to see the Grand Canyon. You book plane tickets, hotel accommodations, and reserve a rental car. You research the hiking trails and determine what to pack based on the weather conditions. You do all the research and the work, and then you don't go on the trip. It is cancelled. You never experience the breathtaking majesty of the Grand Canyon with your family.

Then you repeat it, week after week, year after year, in a restless cycle. A life without Sabbath is like that — working to an end where you never get to relax and enjoy the Lord's spectacular creation with him and your family.

This week, we will explore the life-changing practice of Sabbath. Practicing Sabbath has transformed my life, and I hope it will do the same for you.

Day 1: Discover

Read Gen 2:2.

What did God do on the seventh day of creation?

What does it mean to make something holy?

Why do you think God incorporated a day of rest into the days of creation?

Imagine if God didn't create a holy day of Sabbath rest. What would that say about our world and God?

Creation and Sabbath are intrinsically tied together. Rest is in the very order of creation and of our existence. God created for six days, saw that it was good, and on the seventh day he rested in the beauty he created.

God consecrates the Sabbath and blesses it (Gen 2:1–2). This seventh day is special because God declares it holy. The Hebrew word for holy is "kadosh", meaning "set apart for a sacred purpose."[1] God set apart the Sabbath as a special day for us to enjoy him and his creation. This holy day reminds us that we are not mere

1. Keener and Walton, *Cultural Backgrounds Study Bible*, 4.

machines, built solely for work and productivity. In Gen 1:31, God saw all that he had made and declared it "very good." He enjoys the beauty of the fruits of his labor and is not merely concerned with the production, but with what results from it. Sabbath shows that God is a God of work and rest. He is a God who values contemplation, beauty, and restoration. Many would describe these as the very things that make us human. We receive them as gifts from a good Father who knew the perfect rhythm of life from the very beginning.

We search for restoration in the wrong places. After a session of scrolling on Instagram, I often notice I feel restless and unsatisfied, yet I want to scroll more. It's like a thirst that is never quenched, a hunger never satiated. I know I am not the only one. A recent study found that the typical iPhone user touches their phone 2,617 times a day.[2] We are searching for something that can only be found in the Sabbath rest the Lord gives.

What do you need rest from in your life?

Think about Sabbath as a holy, set-apart day. What does that look like in the context of your own life?

2. Naftulin, "Here's How Many Times We Touch Our Phones Every Day."

Day 2: Discover

Read Exodus 20:8–11.

What does the text specifically say to do about the Sabbath (vs. 8)?

What does it mean to remember the Sabbath?

How could the Israelites specifically keep their Sabbath holy?

Read Deuteronomy 5:12–15.

What active verb is used for Sabbath in this verse?

What does it mean to observe?

What is the difference between remembering the Sabbath and observing the Sabbath?

These passages about the Sabbath are similar, but some nuances reveal how God wanted the Israelite people to observe the Sabbath.

Firstly, these two passages were written to different generations. The book of Exodus was written to the newly- freed Hebrew people, showing them the way of life after slavery. The book of Deuteronomy was written forty years after the generation that had been born into slavery. This second generation was the children of those formerly enslaved people, who had no personal knowledge of the slavery their parents endured.[3]

The keyword in Exodus for the Sabbath is "remember." This generation of people, freed enslaved people, needed help remembering they were the chosen people of God. They were called to remember the Sabbath and keep it holy. "For in six days the Lord made the heavens and the earth, the sea, and all that is in them, but he rested on the seventh day. Therefore, the Lord blessed the Sabbath day and made it holy (Exod 20:11 NIV)."

Notice the reason for God's chosen people to keep the Sabbath. He is calling them back to the creation story. He commands them to remember that the Lord created perfect order and rested. They were once enslaved people living in a broken and harmful society, but now they can rest in the peace of a God who reminds them of the original plan. Sabbath calls us back to the Garden of Eden, long before the serpent ever entered. Sabbath is the invitation to rest like our Father.

Deuteronomy's commandment for the Sabbath is slightly different, calling the Israelites to "observe" it. It goes a step further than remembering. It asks the Israelites to "shamar," or observe, to keep, to put into practice. This command provides the chosen people with guidelines on how to celebrate the holy day, or, as I prefer to think of it, the holiday. Think of the Sabbath as a mini holiday each week. It is like Christmas without all the excessive stress and

3. Comer, "Sabbath as Resistance."

awkward uncles at Christmas dinner. You can observe it through specific rituals, traditional recipes, and decorative elements. The verse continues and commands the people to "remember that you were slaves in Egypt and that the Lord your God brought you out of there with a mighty hand and an outstretched arm. Therefore, the Lord your God has commanded you to observe the Sabbath day (vs. 15 NIV)."

Where Exodus called God's people to be grounded in creation, reminding them only to work six days, Deuteronomy is grounded in freedom, reminding this younger generation of the miraculous work the Lord has done for them. They (and we) are called to observe the Sabbath and to remember the goodness of the Lord God in our lives, setting apart this special day each week.

Both Scriptures command rest at all levels of society. God built a rhythm into the fabric of creation, and so too it would be intrinsic to the lives of his chosen people. The stop day is a relinquishing of control. It is the faith that the Lord, who created the universe and rested on the seventh day, will provide what we need. We realize we cannot accomplish everything. And the loving Father smiles and laughs at his children, saying, "Who told you you are supposed to"? We stop because the Lord stopped. Humans are finite. God is infinite, and still he rested. Like little children who are tucked in to bed by their loving Father, we rest in his power and grace.

What would you like to remember that the Lord has done for you?

What are you slave to?

Day 3: Discover

Read Mark 2:27–28.

What were Jesus' disciples doing as they walked?

Why did the Pharisees say this was unlawful to do on the Sabbath?

What was Jesus' response?

How do you view the Sabbath? Is it a bunch of rules about rest or something else?

In Mark 2, the Pharisees sought to catch Jesus' followers in error, attempting to do so by applying a strict interpretation of the law. Exodus 34:21 (NLT) says, "Six days you shall labor, but on the seventh day you shall rest; even during the plowing season and harvest you must rest." The fact that the Pharisees looked at the disciples' picking of a few heads of grain as harvesting is extreme. Jesus' followers were simply walking with their teacher, having a light snack. They weren't harvesting grain. Israelite law permitted those who were hungry to take grain as they walked through a field. But the Pharisees baulked at the idea of this because it was done on the Sabbath.[4]

4. Keener and Walton, *Cultural Backgrounds Study Bible*, 1689.

Jesus' response to the Pharisees is twofold. He first uses the Scriptures and applies them to the situation. He does this often, showing them their misinterpretation of the very Scriptures they have devoted their lives to. With a question (Haven't you heard?), Jesus mentions how King David did far worse when he was hungry and ate the consecrated bread of the temple.

Then Jesus speaks to the heart of the problem: "The Sabbath was made for man, not man for the Sabbath. So the Son of Man is Lord even over the Sabbath (Mark 2:27 NLT)." Jesus knows their hearts are not turned toward God but to pride in themselves and their knowledge of the Scriptures and the status it brings. Jesus is Lord over the Sabbath, serving humanity and demonstrating that the Sabbath is a blessing, not a burden, as the Pharisees have portrayed it.

Jesus longed to restore the original intent of the Sabbath. The Pharisees had made it about following thousands of little laws to achieve perfection, but that is not what it is about. The Sabbath is a time for us to rest and enjoy.

I believe that if Jesus were to live in our modern times, he would have the same longing to restore the Sabbath to the church. I don't need to tell you that the modern world moves at lightning speed. Once the Industrial Revolution started, the world no longer moved at human pace. It moved at the speed of machines. Further technological advances in those machines, with the invention of computers, smartphones, and Artificial Intelligence, pushed this pace even faster. While there are advantages to this speed, the bigger question is: what is it doing to our souls?

Are we more compassionate because we have technology at our fingertips and know every news story around the world with a simple scroll? Are we more patient with rapid internet speed and endless TikToks to watch? Who are we as people now in this fast-paced world?

Exhausted, anxious, world-weary.

Or worse, we are lonely, depressed, and suicidal.

Many times, after grading papers and answering emails, all the while noticing the pinging of notifications on my phone, I feel like Bilbo Baggins in The Fellowship of the Ring when he tells Gandalf: "I feel thin, sort of stretched, like butter scraped over too much bread."[5]

The constant noise of the modern world doesn't allow us to open up to God, even for a few minutes, let alone an entire day. But that is precisely why we need rest. The world is too overwhelming for us without the practice of the Sabbath. Our creative souls are slowly being drained.

John Ortberg says: "For many of us, the great danger is not that we will renounce our faith. It is that we will become so distracted and rushed and preoccupied that we will settle for a mediocre version of it. We will just skim our lives instead of living them."[6]

We need Jesus, Lord of the Sabbath, to restore our souls.

5. Tolkien, *The Fellowship of the Ring.*

6. Ortberg, *The Life You've Always Wanted*, 38–39.

Day 4: Creative Invitation

Create a Sabbath Ritual

One of the best ways to connect with God the Creator is to observe the Sabbath. Once we allow space for Sabbath, there is space for creativity. Our minds slow their rapid pace, and interesting thoughts start to seep in. The space allows us to listen and connect with God. There is time for us to just be, without obligation.

Sabbath is more than just a day off, where we catch up on yard work, groceries, and laundry. Sabbath invites you to rest and enjoy — to remember and observe. It gives us space to connect with God in a worshipful way, and this includes creating. For the Sabbath, you are simply creating space to worship him.

Today, you will create a Sabbath ritual. This will help you create Sabbath space in your life and determine what you want it to look like. Use the questions, "Is it rest"? and "Is it worship"? as your guide. The responses are different for everyone. I love being out in the garden on the Sabbath, but others might view this as a chore. Reflect on what is restful and worshipful for you personally.

If you are feeling overwhelmed by the idea of taking a whole day off, start small. Consider setting aside time in the morning or afternoon to observe the Sabbath. Then, as you enjoy its benefits in your life, add more time until it is an entire day. Know that it takes time. Give yourself grace, and little by little, you can return to Sabbath rest as you were intended.

Based on your work schedule (primarily if you work in the medical field or for the church), your Sabbath may not be on Sunday or even a weekend. Find another day of the week to rest and make it a priority to do so.

How will you remember the Sabbath and keep it holy? Take out distractions. What will you remove to make this day different from the rest?

Some ideas to get you started:

- Refrain from using your phone/laptop on the Sabbath. (Hide them in your closet!)
- Trade in your smartwatch for an analogue one, or none at all.
- Refrain from household chores (such as laundry).
- Schedule errands, kids' activities, and work meetings for the other six days of the week.

How will you observe the Sabbath and keep it holy? Think celebration. What will you add to your day to make it remarkable?

Some ideas to get you started:

- Light a candle at sundown of your Sabbath to observe its start.
- Attend worship.
- Choose a Sabbath Scripture and read it at the opening or closing of each Sabbath. (Ps 100 is a good start.)
- Create a special Sabbath dinner (this could be a cereal dinner for the kids, a date night for parents, or a special family dessert after dinner, for example).

Complete these journal prompts below to help you be even more specific about your Sabbath.

My Sabbath day starts with:

My Sabbath day ends with:

How I want to connect with God on the Sabbath is:

How I want to connect with my loved ones on the Sabbath is:

The food I want to eat on Sabbath is:

The "busyness" items in my Sabbath that I want to remove are:

Now try it out! Find time in the next few weeks to incorporate these Sabbath rituals into your practice slowly so that you can remember and observe them.

Day 5: Truths and Reflection

Truths to Declare

Each session includes a list of truths learned that week in our study. I invite you to declare them (out loud!) over yourself each day as you study. They are written in the first person so that you can do so.

1. Sabbath rest is ingrained in the creation of our universe (Gen 1–2).
2. I honor the Lord by remembering the Sabbath and keeping it holy (Exod 20:8–11).
3. Jesus helps me remember that Sabbath is for man, not man for the Sabbath (Mark 2:23–28).

Questions for You and the Lord

After reading through God's word and his truths this week, take a moment to reflect on the following questions. These questions are for you and God alone, unless you feel inclined to share them as an encouragement to others.

What truths do you easily believe this week? Why?

What aspects of these truths would you like to explore more?

Ask the Lord what the next steps are for you to Sabbath rest. Is there a calendar item the Lord is bringing to your mind to remove or reschedule?

Day 6: Group Reflection

Group Discussion Questions

As you prepare for your meeting together, answer the following questions to share with the group.

Were there any study questions from Days 1–3 that stood out to you that you would like to discuss?

What is something you want to share with a friend from what you learned this week?

Have you ever practiced the Sabbath before? What did you do or not do on that day?

Creative Group Experience

Your leader will guide you in a creative exercise as a group. After completing the activity, they will guide you to answer the following questions as a group:

What does rest look like or feel like to you?

What activities help you reconnect with God?

How might Sabbath help you recharge physically, emotionally, and spiritually?

Would anyone like to share their mandala and what it means to you and Sabbath?

Leader, please refer to Session 5 Creative Group Experience in the Leader's Guide for instructions.

Close up of *Selah* by Brooke Harris

Session 6

Building His Kingdom

Introduction

It has been recorded that Bach wrote the letters S.D.G. at the bottom of his finished compositions. It stands for the Latin phrase, "Glory to God alone." But at the top of his compositions, before he ever composed a note, he wrote the words, "Jesu Juva", Latin for "Jesus help!"[1]

I am comforted that one of the greatest composers of all time still leaned on Jesus for his creativity. Bach knew that without help from God, it wouldn't be the music he was supposed to compose. Falling flat, the music would lack its purpose and intention.

Relying on Jesus daily, hourly, minute by minute is the posture of a faithful follower of Christ. In this session, we will learn how to bring God's kingdom to a hurting world and explore the significant role creativity plays in this endeavor. We don't do it alone! But first, answer this question:

Like Bach, where are the places in your life where you ask for Jesus' help?

1. Hofreiter, "Johann Sebastian Bach and Scripture," 71.

Day 1: Discover

Read John 9:1–34.

Did the blind man ask for Jesus' healing? Why do you think Jesus healed him?

What "materials" does Jesus use to heal the blind man?

Jesus could have simply spoken over the man to heal him. Why do you think he did otherwise (vs. 13)?

After being healed, how does the blind man show that he is a disciple of Jesus (vs. 27)?

For God's glory, this blind man is healed, and he becomes a follower of Jesus (vs. 27). In the story, the religious leaders do not listen. They are power hungry and threaten people with punishment if they do not follow their commands. See how the blind man's parents are intimidated by them. They do not want to be thrown from the temple. The Pharisees are furious at the fact that this miracle was done on the Sabbath.

Through this healing of the man born physically blind, Jesus shows who is really spiritually blind. He does this through the simple act of making mud. He spits on the ground, and dust becomes mud to smooth over the man's eyes, almost like a salve. The blind man not only sees the light of day but sees the Light of the World!

God's glory is shown in how Kristi McLelland says, "Jesus didn't come to turn things upside down, he came to turn things right side up."[2] As we learned last session, Sabbath is for man, not man for Sabbath.

Jesus is turning things right side up.

The use of mud symbolizes the act of creation. In Genesis, God formed the first man, Adam, from the dust of the ground (mud). By using mud to heal the blind man, Jesus connects himself to the act of creation, emphasizing his divine authority. He was there when Adam was created; he is present and working in the world, healing this blind man.[3]

The Lord often uses the parameters of his creation for his glory. The physicality of this world is a tool and a medium through which he operates. It is this act of creativity that brings his people closer to him. It teaches us and illustrates his goodness.

- Jesus uses waterpots and wine to show the glory of God in his first recorded miracle (John 2:1–11).
- God uses Moses' wooden staff to perform his miracles for the Hebrew people and to demonstrate his power to the Egyptians (Exod 4, 7, 8, 14, 17).
- Jesus places mud on a blind man's eyes to bring humankind closer to him, to believe in him as the Son of Man, the Messiah (John 9:1–34).

The means and mediums are his tools for glory. They are our tools for drawing close to him and giving him that glory.

2. McLellan, *Jesus & Women*, 132.
3. Keener and Walton, *Cultural Backgrounds Study Bible*, 1829.

In his book Art + Faith: A Theology of Making, Makoto Fujimura writes: "God does not need any of our institutions to exist, period, but God's exuberant love invites us, broken vessels of God's choosing, to co-create into the New Creation through Jesus."[4]

Jesus often used unconventional methods to perform miracles, challenging common perceptions of how healing should occur. By using mud, Jesus emphasizes that it is not the method itself but the power of God working through him that brings about healing.[5]

4. Fujimura, *Art + Faith*, 18.

5. Keener and Walton, *Cultural Backgrounds Study Bible*, 1829.

Day 2: Discover

Read Exodus 14:10–31.

What was the situation the Hebrew people were in that they thought was impossible?

What did God instruct Moses to do with the staff (vs. 16)?

God uses what we have to bring his glory. He uses Moses' staff to rescue the Hebrew people. Years later, through the prophet Elisha, he uses the widow's oil to save her life and her son's. We may not think we have a lot to offer him, but that is not the thought that he cares about. God asks: "What do you have? Whatever you have, I can use." He takes our small pieces and sows the miraculous into them to bring life and restoration.

The staff is our starting point. The jar of olive oil is what we offer. Your sketchbook or guitar is the beginning of an incredible adventure with the Creator of the Universe. He uses these things to bring about his good purposes in you. In him, we find this yearning to be our authentic selves who flourish in the Kingdom of a Heavenly King.

What situation have you been in that you thought was impossible?

Verse 31 says, because of the miracle they saw in the parting of the Red Sea, the "Israelites...put their trust in [The Lord] and in Moses his servant."

God invites Moses to partner with him and to lead the Hebrew people to freedom. Moses wasn't overly excited about this. After he made many excuses and requested that his brother, Aaron, join, he finally said "yes" to God. After that "Yes," Moses is given God's power and authority, seen clearly in the miracles he performs. God demonstrates his power first by turning the staff into a snake (Exod 4:2–5). Then Moses evokes the plagues on Egypt after Pharaoh's disobedience and defiance towards God. After raising his staff, Moses, through the power of God, sends a plague of blood, frogs, gnats, and flies (Exod 7:19–8:21).

Again, the Lord could have done the work himself. He simply could have spoken over the Nile, and it would have turned to blood. But he longs for a loving relationship with us. I think having a physical object for Moses to hold on to comforted this shy and self-conscious man. God showed him a sign through a physical object to fill Moses with faith in him.

Sometimes, like the Hebrew people, we see the impossibility of a situation. We look at a sea before us and the army behind us and say, "How is this possible to move through? There is no way to fix this"! But we can start with a prayer of faith.

We can all pray:

"Lord Jesus, how do you want to redeem this situation?"[6]

6. Horrobin, *Healing through Creativity*, 117.

Day 3: Discover

Read Revelation 21:1–7.

What did author John see in verses 21:1–2?

Notice verse 4. What does the Lord do for his people?

What does Christ call himself in verse 6?

What implications does this scripture passage have for you today?

Revelation is a complex book, but we are going to look at it in terms of the New Creation. The Bible begins and ends with creation. The Lord created the heavens and the Earth in Genesis 1, and in Christ's return in Revelation 21, he sits on his throne over the New Heaven and the New Earth.

Jesus is the Beginning and the End, the Alpha and the Omega. What we do between those two bookends is essential.

Notice in verse 4 that it says the Lord "will wipe every tear from their eyes, and there will be no more death or sorrow or crying or pain." Once the New Heaven and New Earth are established, there will be no more suffering! Hallelujah! But here, on this side of that reality, we have tears in our eyes. We have pain in our hearts.

Our friends and family suffer greatly, but they do not suffer alone. In this scene, the people come to the Lord with tears in their eyes, a physical representation of what it means to suffer.

This is where we are today. It is the messy middle, but also an invitation from God to create peace and joy amid the dark reality around us. We are to use the painful experiences of our lives and cultivate his goodness. We grow in maturity through hardship and into a deeper relationship with Jesus, who never leaves us.

In this middle place, we are called to tell the Truth, however beautifully we can. These creative acts are vital because when we step into creativity and engage with our Creator Father with the Holy Spirit, our spirits are renewed and restored.

I don't think it was a coincidence that Jesus grew up in the carpenter trade. He used his hands to create fine artistry. He entered into a creative act and was able to connect with his Father God, which prepared him for ministry.

Creativity with God revitalizes us to return to the weary world and give sacrificially, just as Christ did, to others. Our words and actions matter; what we say and do builds the kingdom, and Jesus uses it to create the holy city of God. St. Augustine is credited with saying: "Without God, we cannot. Without us, God will not."[7]

God longs to bring in his kingdom with us. We can participate only when we know our true identity as creative people redeemed by Christ.

You are a kingdom bringer of the New Creation.

How are you bringing peace/shalom to your small part of the world? What does it look like for you to bring in his kingdom?

7. St. Augustine, "St. Augustine Quotes."

What is God inviting you to do to partner with him in his Kingdom?

What "creative mediums" are needed for this good work?

Day 4: Creative Invitation

For this week's creative invitation, I invite you to do something that uses your imagination. Our imagination is an incredible gift from God, given to us by his good grace.

God's grace is exemplified in many ways: his prevenient grace that covers our lives, his justifying and forgiving grace as Christ's sacrifice on the cross, and his empowering and regenerating grace that he gives us to build his kingdom.

Your imagination, explicitly given by him, is a part of that grace.

Think about how you would like to use your imagination to connect with God. This could be writing poetry, doodling, playing an instrument, knitting, journaling, painting with watercolors, or collaging. Please don't feel obligated to spend a significant amount of time on this, as it tends to discourage us from starting.

Set a timer for ten minutes if you would like. The purpose is to connect with God. Play calming music if you are not playing an instrument yourself. If you need a suggestion, Cageless Birds's song "Art of Connection" is a good one.

Create while reflecting on our question from yesterday's teaching:

What does it look like for you to bring in his kingdom?

Day 5: Truths and Reflection

Truths to Declare

Each session includes a list of truths learned that week in our study. I invite you to declare them (out loud!) over yourself each day as you study. They are written in the first person so that you can do so.

1. I am creative because my Heavenly Father is the Creator (Gen 1:27).
2. Jesus rose from the dead and launched the new creation, on Earth as it is in Heaven (Luke 17:21).
3. What I do now brings a piece of God's new creation to a suffering world (Acts 1:8).

Questions for You and the Lord

After reading through God's word and his truths this week, take a moment to reflect on the following questions. These questions are for you and God alone, unless you feel inclined to share them as an encouragement to others.

What truths do you easily believe this week? Why?

What truths are difficult to accept? Why?

What aspects of these truths would you like to explore more?

Day 6: Group Reflection

Group Discussion Questions

As you prepare for your meeting together, answer the following questions to share with the group.

Were there any study questions from Days 1–3 that stood out to you that you would like to discuss?

What is something you want to share with a friend from what you learned this week?

What does it mean to bring in God's Kingdom?

Creative Group Experience

Your leader will guide you in a creative exercise as a group. After completing the activity, your leader will guide you to journal responses to the following questions:

What do you notice about your collage? Is there a particular theme, recurring pattern, or color?

What thoughts or emotions did you experience as you created your collage?

What is your favorite image/word in your collage and why?

Leader, please refer to Session 6 Creative Group Experience in the Leader's Guide for instructions.

Meet a Fellow Creator: Antje Smith, who inspired this collage experience.

Antje Smith is an artist and mother who loves showing people how to live a creative life. Through her collage workshops and artistic expressions, she shares how creativity helps her process life experiences and connect with God in everyday life. Follow her at @ safehaven_art.

Photograph of paintbrushes, credit: Brooke Harris

A Closing Benediction

Group Leader, read this over the study participants as they open their hands to receive it at the end of your final session meeting:

How wonderful You made us, Lord. Our bodies bring forth your creation. They hold the very life itself that you give us. How amazing it is to be your child – that you created us out of extravagant Love, needing nothing from us. We love you wholeheartedly.

Thank you, Lord, for always being with us even when we are not quiet enough to hear You. We ask for forgiveness for believing the lie that You are not here, and You do not speak. We know that You are the Creator of the universe, and You still speak to us! Help us to quiet our minds and our environments so that we can listen to You clearly. Protect us from distractions and lies that send us farther from You. Thank you for inviting us to partner with you and with each other. We long to be your unified church. You have made us all unique parts of a perfected body in Christ Jesus. Show us the role that you have for us. Thank you for Jesus, who, through his sacrifice and grace, enables us to move towards maturity and perfection.

Teach us, Lord, how to use the good gifts you have given us to bring in your Kingdom. Remind us of our creativity and how it connects us to you and your people. Please help us to be tender–hearted to those who need to know you. Send your Holy Spirit into our hearts, lives, and homes so that we may shine your light throughout the world. Amen.

Leader's Guide

Session 1

Creative Group Experience: A Messy Drawing

Objective:

Participants will create a layered mixed-media artwork that symbolizes their identity and uniqueness within God's creation, experiencing a hands-on reflection on being known, loved, and chosen by him.

Calming music in the background is helpful for these creative exercises. You can play "soaking" music on YouTube or a relaxing playlist of your own. Usually, music without lyrics is helpful as people are listening to God, and you don't want the words to distract from participants' thoughts.

Supplies:

- white printer paper
- 8.5 x 11 white cardstock paper (one per person)
- masking tape
- A variety of drawing utensils (crayons, markers, pastels, colored pencils). It does not matter what type but having a variety of supplies allows people to add layers to their piece.
- colorful paper scraps
- glue sticks
- Scissors (people can share)

The following steps are written to the participant so leaders can read them aloud to the group easily:

Step One

On the printer paper, write all the aspects of your identity – what you like to do, who you are in your family, and what your name means if you know the meaning. Write all the words you can think of to get ideas flowing.

Step Two

After brainstorming, choose a symbol that illustrates you. It could be a small fish, a bird, or a flower. Choose something that feels like you. Draw the simple shape on the masking tape and then cut it out. Place the tape in the center of your painting. Press firmly.

Step Three

Choose three to four colors of drawing supplies and swipe the color on your paper. Choose colors that you enjoy and are the most like you, colors you are drawn to. Make sure to color over your masking tape shape without coloring under the tape.

Step Four

Now create a "mess" with your drawing materials. Continue to layer colors with different mediums. Be creative by adding dashes, strokes, and dots, and layering for added interest. More layers represent the vastness and variety of God's creation.

Step Five

Use cut-up paper if you choose to add textural elements. Glue them on your paper.

Step Six

Let your mixed media piece dry for a few minutes, then peel off the taped symbol that represents you. Through all the vastness of creation, God knows and loves you. You are loved by him, chosen to create.

Step Seven

Discuss your experience with the group. You do not have to go into the personal details of what the Lord shared with you, only if you would like. Use the following questions to guide your discussion:

- After creating your "messy" drawing, what was the most enjoyable part about creating it? Why?
- Did the act of layering lots of different colors, patterns, and textures feel freeing or overwhelming? Why?
- How would you act differently if you walked every day of your life with a complete sense of God wanting you as his child?

Session 2

Creative Group Experience: Painting our Emotions

Objective:

(Inspired by Cultivate No. 1, "The Head to Heart Journey.")[1] Participants will use watercolor to visually express their emotions, inviting God into the creative process to transform head knowledge into heartfelt connection.

Calming music in the background is helpful for these creative exercises. You can play "soaking" music on YouTube or a relaxing playlist of your own. Usually, music without lyrics is helpful as people are listening to God, and you don't want the words to distract from participants' thoughts.

Supplies:

- white printer paper
- watercolor paper
- watercolors
- paint brushes
- water/cups
- paper towels

The following steps are written to the participant so leaders can read them aloud to the group easily.

Step One

Take a deep breath and slow down. Ask yourself: "What am I feeling right now"? Write down three to five emotions in a journal or on printer paper and then assign them each a color. There is

1. Helser, "The Head to Heart Journey."

no right or wrong color. Choose whatever you associate with that emotion.

Step Two

Now dip your brush into the water and spread the water all over your watercolor paper. Let the paper become damp, but not sopping. Starting with your lightest color, add water to the designated colors in your pan that correspond to the emotions you have assigned. Drop the color onto your damp paper, letting the colors pool and move. You can paint simple shapes or lines. If it is too dry, add more water.

Move on to the following colors, adding drops of color onto your paper. Colors can blend and remember you aren't painting a realistic picture. Use all colors that represent your emotions. While you paint, speak to the Lord about the emotions you are expressing through your painting. Be honest and pray using all the feelings you identified in step one.

Step Three

After you are done painting, allow God to respond to your prayer. Journal God's words that speak to your heart. Answer this question in his voice: "God, what are your thoughts and feelings about me right now"?

Step Four

Discuss your experience with the group. You do not have to go into the personal details of what the Lord shared with you, only if you would like. Use the following questions to guide your discussion:

- What colors did you choose for your emotions, and why?
- Did your colors blend or touch? What about that did you like or dislike?

- Was there anything significant in the act of creating that struck you?
- Emotionally, what feelings are blending and confusing for you?

Session 3

Creative Group Experience: Resistance Painting

Objective:

Participants will explore the contrast between resistance and receptivity through a watercolor and crayon exercise, reflecting on how surrendering to the Holy Spirit allows God to move freely and create beauty from our own paths and brokenness.

Calming music in the background is helpful for these creative exercises. You can play "soaking" music on YouTube or a relaxing playlist of your own. Usually, music without lyrics is helpful as people are listening to God, and you don't want the words to distract from participants' thoughts.

Supplies:

- white printer paper
- pencils
- white crayons
- watercolor paper
- watercolors and brushes
- water/cups

The following steps are written to the participant so leaders can read them aloud to the group easily.

Step One

On the printer paper, loosen up by scribbling with a pencil. Make your own mark. Create a repetitive design – one with straight lines or one with curves.

Step Two

With a white crayon, draw your design on the watercolor paper. This can be a simple line or scribble since you will not be able to see it. Think about pressing in firmly. It is okay if the crayon breaks. We create our own marks and paths. Consider how difficult this feels, how resistant the crayon is on the paper.

Step Three

Add watercolors to your design. Use colors you are drawn to. Two to three is sufficient. Notice that adding water creates less resistance. It is eager to move and is receptive. God uses our brokenness. After we stop resisting his love, he moves throughout our lives creating beauty. We can see the paths we've taken and tried to move on our own, and we can see God's encompassing love over it all. Jesus was the perfect no–resistance home for the Holy Spirit. He did community and solitude well. That constant push and pull of living in community and seeking the father alone created a rhythm for his life.

Step Four

Discuss your experience with the group. You do not have to go into the personal details of what the Lord shared with you, only if you would like. Use the following questions to guide your discussion:

- What happened when the watercolors interacted with the white crayon?
- Where do you see yourself resisting the Holy Spirit?
- Do you naturally gravitate toward community or solitude?
- How is the Holy Spirit calling you to the one that is not your natural bent?

Session 4

Creative Group Experience: Writing A Psalm

Objective: Participants will write their own personal psalms, using creative journaling to express the emotions of their body, mind, and heart before God.

Calming music in the background is helpful for these creative exercises. You can play "soaking" music on YouTube or a relaxing playlist of your own. Usually, music without lyrics is helpful as people are listening to God, and you don't want the words to distract from participants' thoughts.

Supplies

- journals or printer paper
- pencils
- Bibles

The following steps are written to the participant so leaders can read them aloud to the group easily.

Step One

I need a few volunteers to read the following Psalms passages aloud. As they read, let's have the rest of the group identify which emotions are present.

- Psalm 100:1–5 – Joy
- Psalm 42 – Despair/depression
- Psalm 108:1–5 – Gratitude/confidence/joy
- Psalm 13 – Loneliness

Step Two

Journal your own psalm. Write down some keywords of what you are feeling right now through different parts of yourself. Journal these questions:

- What is your body feeling? (achy, sore, strong, etc.)
- How is your mind doing at this moment? (anxious, overwhelmed, sharp, inspired)
- What is your heart feeling right now? (grateful, sad, etc.)

Step Three

Now assign a word to each part of yourself: body, mind and heart. You will end up with three emotions, one for each part of you. For example: strong body, an anxious mind, and a loving heart.

Step Four

Write a metaphor or simile for each of your identified body, heart, mind emotions.

- A simile compares two things using 'like' or 'as'. Example: my calm mind is like a pane of glass, transparent and open.
- A metaphor compares without using like or as. Example: my anxious heart is a freight train. This is a brainstorming free–write exercise and does not need to be perfect. The idea is to share these emotions with the Lord in a creative outlet.

Step Five

Add to your metaphors and similes. You can create a stanza or a small paragraph for each part: body, mind, and heart. You can start each section with a simile or a metaphor. Free write without judging the writing just yet.

Step Six

Spend a few minutes reading over your poem/journaling exercise and condense your words. You may want to consolidate your work into a smaller, more cohesive poem. Organize your writing into a psalm – a simple piece of writing that expresses your emotions. Tell God what you feel honestly. These psalms will not be shared unless you would like to share them. Answer these questions as a group:

- Which stanza did you like the best in your composition and why? What did it represent (body, mind, heart)?
- Which emotion was the most difficult to convey through words? Why?
- How was it healing to write your emotions before the Lord?

Session 5

Creative Group Experience: Creating a Sabbath Mandala

Objective:

Mandalas have been used for centuries by various religions as a means of meditation and spiritual practice. For this activity, participants will create a Sabbath mandala and meditate on the restorative power of the Sabbath. Craft Wack's simple mandala example inspired the instructions for this activity.[2]

Calming music in the background is helpful for these creative exercises. You can play "soaking" music on YouTube or a relaxing playlist of your own. Usually, music without lyrics is helpful as people are listening to God, and you don't want the words to distract from participants' thoughts.

Supplies

- paper plates to trace circles (need to be small enough to trace on 8.5 x 11 in. sheets of printer paper)
- white printer paper
- scissors
- pencils with erasers
- spoon or other hard object to crease the paper
- fine tip markers, gel pens, or colored pencils

The following steps are written to the participant so leaders can read them aloud to the group easily.

2. Gonzales, "How to Draw Simple Beautiful Mandalas."

Step One

Begin by creating a circle by tracing a paper plate on to your paper. After drawing a circle, cut it out with scissors.

Step Two

Fold the circle in half. Then fold it in half again. Finally, fold it in half again. You should have a folded piece of paper resembling a pie piece.

Step Three

Focus on this question: What activities help you connect back to God? Journal your answers and pick a symbol for these activities to use in your mandala design. You might draw a golf club for recreation or a whisk to represent baking. With a pencil, add the symbol in the center of the pie piece. Then, add repeated designs around the symbol to fill the pie piece, ensuring the lines touch the edges of the paper so that they will connect when opened. This can be a repetitive decorative design. After drawing the design, trace over it with a pencil, making your marks heavy and dark.

Step Four

After drawing your design, use the existing crease and fold the drawn pie piece over onto the piece next to it. Then, rub the back of a spoon (or another firm object) over the pencil marks to transfer them onto the blank pie piece. Press firmly! Go over the transfer lines with your pencil to darken them. Fold these two pieces over onto the neighboring two pieces and repeat the rubbing and darkening process. Fold these four onto the blank four pieces and repeat the transfer. Darken the transferred lines with a pencil until you have a completed mandala.

Step Five

Color your mandala with colors you enjoy and are drawn to. Slow your hand and mind being ready for reflection. Invite the Holy Spirit to help you reflect on this question: "What does rest look like or feel like to you"?

Step Six

After coloring in your mandala and journaling, discuss these questions in a group:

- What does rest look like or feel like to you?
- What activities help you reconnect with God?
- How might Sabbath help you recharge physically, emotionally, and spiritually.

Session 6

Creative Group Experience: Identity Collage

Objective:

Participants will create a personal collage that visually expresses their inner life and emotions, using intuitive imagery and reflection to experience God's unconditional love.

This last session will be a time of reflection and celebration. You may want to allow for an extended period (perhaps an additional thirty minutes) for people to eat and fellowship together. For this last meeting, invite participants to bring in items for a community charcuterie board. You can send out an email or a simple digital sign–up. People can bring in meats, cheeses, crackers, fruit, nuts, and chocolate. Display the food on large platters or parchment paper. Have everyone partake and eat a meal together.

Have each participant bring in a few magazines to share and scissors if you need extra pairs. National Geographic and design magazines often have great images.

Calming music in the background is helpful for these creative exercises. You can play "soaking" music on YouTube or a relaxing playlist of your own. Usually, music without lyrics is helpful as people are listening to God, and you don't want the words to distract from participants' thoughts.

Supplies:

- magazines
- scissors
- 8.5 x 11 cardstock (one for each participant)
- glue sticks

The following steps are written to the participant so leaders can read them aloud to the group easily.

Step One

Look through the magazines and select ten to twenty images or words that come to mind quickly and spontaneously. Tear or cut the page out and allow your imagery to feel mysterious. Do not interpret while you work. Be quiet in the unknowing. Trust the process and see what you are drawn to. You may not yet have words for your emotions. Images speak before words. Find patterns and colors you are intuitively drawn to.

If helpful, keep a prompt in mind, such as:

- How am I doing today?
- What am I ready to invite into my life?
- What am I looking forward to this month?

Step Two

After gathering your images or words, revisit each piece and ask what it is that spoke to you about it. Cut things straighter or smaller if you feel led to a specific part.

- Keep moving.
- Sort them as they feel right to you.
- Group them by color or feel.
- See if one or two pieces stand out more than others.

Step Three

Then begin playing with composition. Lay each piece on the cardstock as it feels right. Feel free to leave some out. You don't have to use all of them. Be open to surprises and go with the flow. Tip: Don't be afraid to add dark images. They may represent parts of yourself you are afraid to share. Be courageous and allow all parts of you to come to the surface to be loved by your Father. Fiona Horrobin says: "We all have shadows but to dismiss these things is to live our lives in a degree of unreality… we need shadows to bring out the color and light."[3] Don't worry about being tidy. Let yourself get lost in the practice of making. Let every part be witnessed, loved, and accepted. Rest in God's love.

Step Four

After playing with the composition and rearranging if needed, glue your final pieces to the paper. The first piece you glue down is often the hardest moment. Consider it an opportunity for courage. It may also feel arbitrary. Either way, pick up the glue stick and commit to it. Start by committing to just one piece if it's hard. Trust you can keep building from there. Be mindful that the final collage sometimes feels slightly different from the one you composed. That's normal. Trust the process and be open to changes. Meditate on your collage and know God's love for every part of you.

Step Five

Journal these questions:

- What do you notice about your collage? Is there a particular theme, recurring pattern or color?
- What thoughts or emotions did you experience as you created your collage?
- What is your favorite image/word in your collage and why?

3. Horrobin, *Healing Through Creativity*, 281.

Step Six

Write your name and the date on the back of the collage. This is important and often overlooked.

Step Seven

As a group, place your collages on a table or white board to share. Notice similarities and differences. You are invited to share your experiences and the observations you made while creating your piece. Move the collages in a different pattern to see how the composition changes when pieces of it are rearranged. Notice that God shapes us and transforms us into his church. We are moving to maturity and arranging ourselves into his people. Put your collage in a special place where you will see it often. Spots like a window ledge, a dresser top, the inside wall of a closet, or the kitchen refrigerator tend to work nicely.

Bibliography

Arnold, Bill T. "Genesis." In *One Volume Commentary*, edited by Kenneth J. Collins and Robert W. Wall., 5. Nashville: Abingdon, 2020.

Case, Joel. "Common Barriers When Journaling the Voice of the Lord." In *Cultivate: The Process of Living from Your Heart*, vol. 1, 22–25. 2023.

Comer, John Mark. "Listening to God." *John Mark Comer Teachings*, December 1, 2023. Podcast.

Comer, John Mark. "Sabbath as Resistance." *John Mark Comer Teachings*, July 19, 2024. Podcast.

Fujimura, Makoto. *Art + Faith: A Theology of Making.* New Haven: Yale University Press, 2021.

Galloway, Emily. "Hearing God's Voice." Lecture presented in Lexington, KY, 2009.

Gaultiere, Bill. "How to Do Lectio Divina." *Soul Shepherding. https://www.soulshepherding.org/lectio-divina-guides/*

Gonzales, Joanne. "How to Draw Simple Beautiful Mandalas." Craft Wack. https://craftwack.com/easy-mandalas

Helser, Jonathan David. "The Head to Heart Journey." *Cultivate: The Process of Living from Your Heart*, vol. 1. 2023.

Hofreiter, Paul. "Johann Sebastian Bach and Scripture." *Concordia Theological Quarterly* 59, nos. 1–2 (1995) 71, http://ctsfw.net/media/pdfs/hofreiterjsbachandscripture.pdf.

Holy Bible, New International Version. Grand Rapids: Zondervan, 2011.

Holy Bible, New Living Translation. Carol Stream, IL: Tyndale House, 2015.

Horrobin, Fiona. *Healing through Creativity.* Lancaster: Sovereign World Ltd, 2020.

Keener, Craig S., and John H. Walton, eds. *Cultural Backgrounds Study Bible: New International Version.4, 1698, 1829,* Grand Rapids: Zondervan, 2016.

Lewis, C. S. *Letters to Malcolm: Chiefly on Prayer.* New York: Harcourt, Brace & World, 1964.

McLellan, Kristi. *Jesus & Women: In the First Century and Now.* Nashville: Lifeway, 2019.

Medium. "The End of Education." https://medium.com/@connect_75384/the-end-of-education-94f3a39fe97c

Merriam-Webster.com Dictionary. *s.v.* "create." https://www.merriam-webster.com/dictionary.create.

"Milky Way," Western Washington University Physics/Astronomy Dept., https://www.wwu.edu/astro101/a101_milkyway.shtml.

Naftulin, Julia. "Here's How Many Times We Touch Our Phones Every Day." *Business Insider*, July 13, 2016. https://www.businessinsider.com/dscout-research-people-touch-cell-phones-2617-times-a-day-2016–7.

Ortberg, John. *The Life You've Always Wanted: Spiritual Disciplines of Ordinary People*. Grand Rapids, MI: Zondervan, 2002.

Smith, David Fenton. "Mark." In *One Volume Commentary*, edited by Kenneth J. Collins and Robert W. Wall, 599. Nashville: Abingdon, 2020.

Sopher, Philip. "Where the FiveDay Workweek Came From." *The Atlantic*, August 21, 2014. https://www.theatlantic.com/business/archive/2014/08/wherethefivedayworkweekcamefrom/378870/.

Staton, Tyler. *Praying Like Monks, Living Like Fools*. Grand Rapids: Zondervan, 2022.

St. Augustine. "St. Augustine Quotes." *quotefancy.com*, January 29, 2025. https://quotefancy.com/St-Augustine-quotes.

Tipp City Church of the Nazarene. "Mother Teresa on Prayer." *Tipp City Church of the Nazarene*. https://www.tcnaz.com/notes/2019/02/27/motherteresaonprayer/.

Tolkien, J. R. R. *The Fellowship of the Ring*. Boston: Mariner Books/Houghton Mifflin Harcourt, 2021.

www.ingramcontent.com/pod-product-compliance
Lightning Source LLC
LaVergne TN
LVHW012331100826
845148LV00017B/2105

* 9 7 9 8 3 8 5 2 7 3 3 3 1 *